IMPERIAL WAR MUSEUMS
COLOURING BOOK

The arrival of the First World War in 1914 changed people's lives around the world, affecting everything from work and attitudes to everyday essentials such as food and clothing. The Imperial War Museum (IWM) was set up in 1917 to document the experiences of soldiers and the people at home who worked to support them. The museum began collecting material from battlefields, factories, and homes while obtaining artworks by Britain's official war artists, some of whom had already been to battle themselves.

Just a few decades later, in 1939, the Second World War began and the museum expanded its mission, ready once more to record the lives of the people involved. Official war artists, commissioned by the government, were asked to draw and paint the war at home and abroad. Meanwhile, vulnerable objects and artworks were moved from the museum to safer locations outside London. Because of this, when the museum was bombed during the Blitz of 1940, many of the exhibits survived. By the end of the Second World War, Britain's artists had created thousands of artworks, many of which came to the museum.

Today these artworks are an important part of history. They help us understand those difficult, life-changing times and connect us to the lives and stories of people who experienced them.

Pomegranate **Kids**®
— AGES 3 to 103!

PARTNERSHIP WITH

IWM
IMPERIAL WAR MUSEUMS

All artworks are in the collections of the Imperial War Museums.

Paintings from the First World War

1. *An Aerial Fight*, 1918. Louis Weirter (1873–1932). Oil on canvas, 236.2 x 205.7 cm (93 x 81 in.). © IWM (Art.IWM ART 654)

2. *Spring in the Trenches, Ridge Wood*, 1917. Paul Nash (1889–1946). Oil on canvas, 60.9 x 50.8 cm (24 x 20 in.). © IWM (Art.IWM ART 1154)

3. *Indian Army Wounded in Hospital in the Dome, Brighton*, 1919. Douglas Fox-Pitt (1864–1922). Oil on canvas, 60.9 x 50.8 cm (24 x 20 in.). © IWM (Art.IWM ART 323)

4. *R34 and R29 in the Shed at East Fortune*, 1919. Alfred Egerton Cooper (1883–1974). Oil on canvas, 60.9 x 91.4 cm (24 x 36 in.). © IWM (Art.IWM ART 4086)

5. *Heavy Artillery*, 1919. Colin Gill (1892–1940). Oil on canvas, 182.8 x 317.5 cm (72 x 125 in.). © IWM (Art.IWM ART 2274)

6. *On the Departure Platform, Victoria Station*, 1918. Bernard Meninsky (1891–1950). Oil on canvas, 91.4 x 71.1 cm (36 x 28 in.). © IWM (Art.IWM ART 1188)

7. *Oppy Wood, 1917. Evening*, 1918. John Nash (1893–1977). Oil on canvas, 182.8 x 213.3 cm (72 x 84 in.). © IWM (Art.IWM ART 2243)

8. *Voluntary Land Workers in a Flax-Field, Podington, Northamptonshire*, 1919. Randolph Schwabe (1885–1948). Oil on canvas, 106.6 x 152.4 cm (42 x 60 in.). © IWM (Art.IWM ART 2288)

9. *The Sea of Galilee: Aeroplanes Attacking Turkish Boats*, 1919. Sydney W. Carline (1888–1929). Oil on canvas, 76.2 x 91.4 cm (30 x 36 in.). © IWM (Art.IWM ART 3080)

10. *Observation of Fire*, 1919. Colin Gill (1892–1940). Oil on canvas, 76.2 x 50.8 cm (30 x 20 in.). © IWM (Art.IWM ART 2297)

11. *Regimental Band*, 1918. Darsie Japp (1883–1973). Oil on panel, 91.4 x 71.1 cm (36 x 28 in.). © IWM (Art.IWM ART 4031)

12. *A French Highway*, 1918. John Nash (1893–1977). Oil on canvas, 91.4 x 71.1 cm (36 x 28 in.). © IWM (Art.IWM ART 1162)

13. *Erecting a Camouflage Tree*, 1919. Leon Underwood (1890–1975). Oil on canvas, 106.6 x 152.4 cm (42 x 60 in.). © IWM (Art.IWM ART 2283)

Paintings from the Second World War

14. *Fighter Affiliation: Halifax and Hurricane Aircraft Co-operating in Action*, 1943. Walter Thomas Monnington (1902–1976). Oil on canvas, 46.3 x 41.2 cm (18¼ x 16¼ in.). © IWM (Art.IWM ART LD 3769)

15. *Tempests Attacking Flying-Bombs*, 1944. Walter Thomas Monnington (1902–1976). Oil on canvas, 90.1 x 114.3 cm (35½ x 45 in.). © IWM (Art.IWM ART LD 4588)

16. *Southern England, 1944. Spitfires Attacking Flying-Bombs*, 1944. Walter Thomas Monnington (1902–1976). Oil on canvas, 105.4 x 143.3 cm (41½ x 56⁷⁄₁₆ in.). © IWM (Art.IWM ART LD 4589)

17. *Building a Battleship*, 1940. Charles Ginner (1878–1952). Oil on canvas, 83.8 x 60.9 cm (33 x 24 in.). © IWM (Art.IWM ART LD 252)

18. *Training – Aircraft Under Construction*, 1940. Raymond McGrath (1903–1977). Watercolour on paper, 55.7 x 37.9 cm (21¹⁵⁄₁₆ x 14¹⁵⁄₁₆ in.). © IWM (Art.IWM ART LD 65)

19. *Parachutes*, 1941. Eric Kennington (1888–1960). Pastel on paper, 73.6 x 53.3 cm (29 x 21 in.). © IWM (Art.IWM ART LD 1259)

20. *A Balloon Site, Coventry*, 1943. Laura Knight (1877–1970). Oil on canvas, 102.5 x 127 cm (40⅜ x 50 in.). © IWM (Art.IWM ART LD 2750)

21. *An Air Gunner in Action Turret: Night*, 1940. Keith Henderson (1883–1982). Oil on canvas, 76.2 x 101.9 cm (30 x 40⅛ in.). © IWM (Art.IWM ART LD 633)

Pomegranate Communications, Inc.
19018 NE Portal Way, Portland OR 97230
800 227 1428   www.pomegranate.com

Colour reproductions © 2014 Imperial War Museums
Line drawings © Pomegranate Communications, Inc.
Sales of this product support the work of IWM.
iwm.org.uk

Item No. CB164

Designed by Carey Hall. Line drawings by Becky Holtzman.

Printed in Korea

23 22 21 20 19 18 17 16 15 14   10 9 8 7 6 5 4 3 2 1

Distributed by Pomegranate Europe Ltd.
Unit 1, Heathcote Business Centre, Hurlbutt Road
Warwick, Warwickshire CV34 6TD, UK
[+44] 0 1926 430111
sales@pomeurope.co.uk

1. *An Aerial Fight*, Louis Weirter

2. *Spring in the Trenches, Ridge Wood*, Paul Nash

3. Indian Army Wounded in Hospital in the Dome, Brighton, Douglas Fox-Pitt

4. *R34 and R29 in the Shed at East Fortune*, Alfred Egerton Cooper

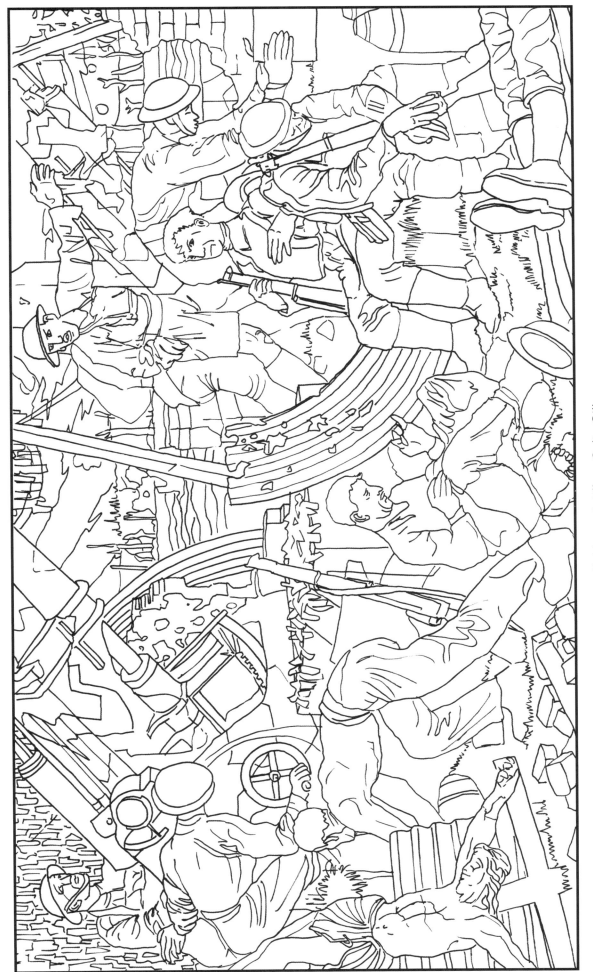

5. Heavy Artillery, Colin Gill

6. *On the Departure Platform, Victoria Station*, Bernard Meninsky

7. Oppy Wood, 1917. Evening, John Nash

8. Voluntary Land Workers in a Flax-Field, Podington, Northamptonshire, Randolph Schwabe

9. The Sea of Galilee: Aeroplanes Attacking Turkish Boats, Sydney W. Carline

10. *Observation of Fire*, Colin Gill

11. *Regimental Band*, Darsie Japp

12. *A French Highway*, John Nash

13. *Erecting a Camouflage Tree, Leon Underwood*

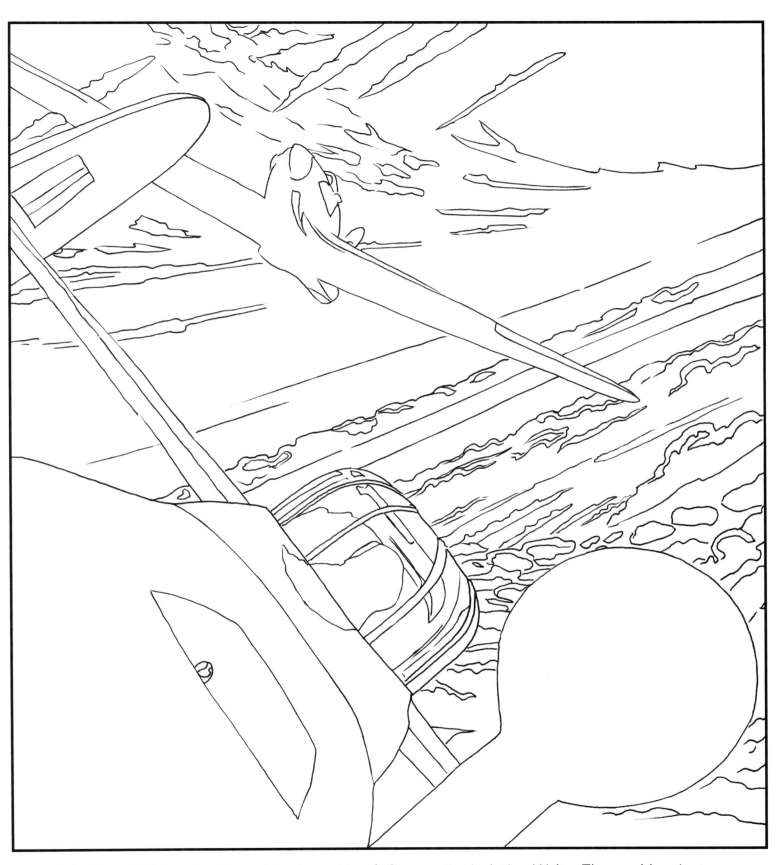

14. *Fighter Affiliation: Halifax and Hurricane Aircraft Co-operating in Action*, Walter Thomas Monnington

15. *Tempests Attacking Flying-Bombs*, Walter Thomas Monnington

16. Southern England, 1944. Spitfires Attacking Flying-Bombs, Walter Thomas Monnington

17. *Building a Battleship*, Charles Ginner

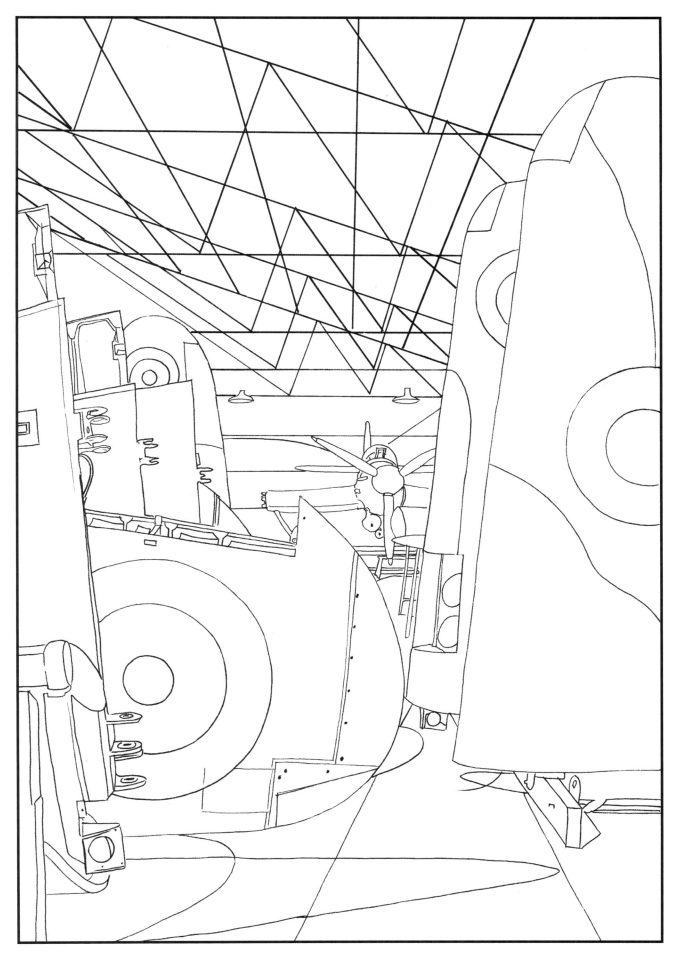

18. *Training – Aircraft Under Construction*, Raymond McGrath

19. *Parachutes*, Eric Kennington

20. *A Balloon Site, Coventry*, Laura Knight

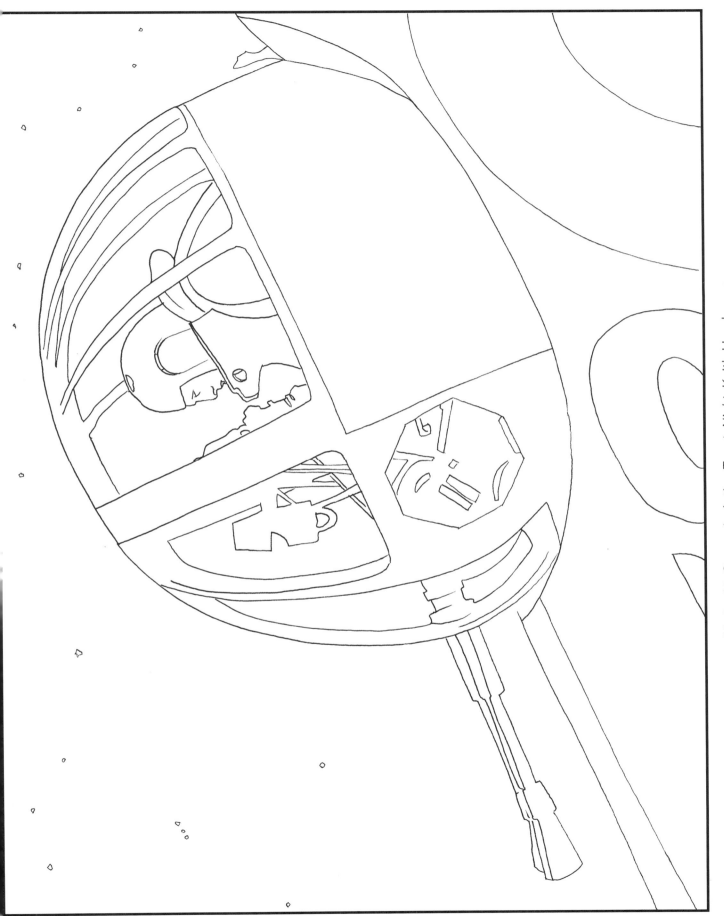

21. *An Air Gunner in Action Turret: Night*, Keith Henderson

Draw and colour your own picture here!

Draw and colour your own picture here!